Sunrise, Sunset, and Seasons

T0021372

Printed in China

ISBN   978-0-358-39156-2

1 2 3 4 5 6 7 8 9 10   0940   30 29 28 27 26 25 24 23 22 21

4500818586

r12.20

Anissa and her brother were playing outdoors when they heard their grandmother calling to them.

"Children! It is getting dark. Time to come indoors."

Anissa and Ravi came in the house. Anissa glanced at the clock.

"But Nani," she said, "it's only 5 o'clock in the afternoon. We can play outside later than this."

"Only in the summer," said Nani. "It is still light at 5 o'clock then."

Anissa frowned and asked, "Why does it get dark earlier in winter?"

"Let's find out tomorrow," said Nani. "It is almost time for dinner, so please help Ravi set the table."

The next day, Nani and Anissa discussed Anissa's question.

Nani said, "You asked why it gets dark earlier in winter. Are you absolutely sure that is true? How could you find out?"

Anissa looked out the window and gave it some thought.

Anissa said, "I know that daylight is light from the sun. We could measure the amount of daylight in a day. But how?"

Nani smiled. "Let's make a plan."

Anissa and Nani made a plan. They would record the time that daylight starts, and they would also record when daylight ends.

Anissa made a drawing of her cat and taped it to a window.

	Sunrise	Sunset
Day 1	7:00 a.m.	5:15 p.m.
Day 2	6:59 a.m.	5:16 p.m.
Day 3	6:58 a.m.	5:17 p.m.
Day 4	6:57 a.m.	5:18 p.m.
Day 5	6:56 a.m.	5:19 p.m.

In the morning, Anissa recorded when there was enough sunlight to see the cat drawing. She also recorded when it was too dark to see the drawing. She did this for five days.

"Nani," said Anissa. "I see that the amount of daylight changes a little from day to day. But this is winter. I know that it gets dark later in summer. Does daylight start and end at different times in different seasons?"

"Think about what you already know," said Nani.

Anissa said, "Every day does not have the same amount of sunlight. I know there are four seasons. Which season has the most daylight?"

"Let's find out," said Nani. "We can use the computer to look for information."

Anissa made a list of the seasons. She would record sunrise and sunset times for a day in each season.

Anissa got a calendar and chose a day in each season. She and Nani looked up what time the sun will seem to rise on that day. They looked up what time the sun will seem to set on that day.

Nani explained how to count the hours from sunrise to sunset.

She said, "Suppose sunrise is at 7 o'clock in the morning and sunset is at 5 o'clock in the afternoon. That is 10 hours of daylight."

	Sunrise	Sunset	Daylight Hours
winter day	7:30 a.m.	4:30 p.m.	9 hours
spring day	6:15 a.m.	6:15 p.m.	12 hours
summer day	5:30 a.m.	7:30 p.m.	14 hours
fall day	6:00 a.m.	7:00 p.m.	11 hours

Anissa looked at her chart. "I see that summer has the most daylight. Sunrise is earlier and sunset is later. Winter has the least daylight. Sunrise is later and sunset is earlier."

Nani said, "Yes, less sunlight means the days seem shorter. But remember that a winter day and a summer day have the same number of hours."

Anissa made a claim. "The amount of daylight changes from season to season." She held up her chart. "Here is my evidence. Summer has more daylight than the other three seasons, and the sun sets earlier in winter. There is less daylight in winter."

Nani smiled and said, "And that is why you and Ravi can play outdoors later on a summer day."

Anissa ran to put on her coat. "Ravi! We should play outside while we can. Soon it will be too dark. But just wait until summer!"